POETRY AFTER 9/11

POETRY AFTER 9/11

AN ANTHOLOGY OF NEW YORK POETS

INTRODUCTION
BY ALICIA OSTRIKER

EDITED BY
DENNIS LOY JOHNSON
AND
VALERIE MERIANS

MELVILLE HOUSE
HOBOKEN, NEW JERSEY
2002

Copyright 2002 Dennis Loy Johnson and Valerie Merians
Introduction copyright, Alicia Ostriker, 2002
Copyright to the poems are held by the individual poets.

Three of the poems in this book first appeared in other publications:
"The World Trade Center" by David Lehman in Valentine Place, Scribner, 1996
"Free Mercy" by Philip Schultz in The New Yorker
"Early, Late" by Philip Fried in Barrow Street
The editors are grateful to the poets and the publications
for allowing us to reprint these poems.

Design: Deb Wood
Melville House Publishing
P.O. Box 3278
Hoboken, NJ 07030

ISBN 0-9718659-1-4

FIRST EDITION

LIBRARY OF CONGRESS
CATALOGING-IN-PUBLICATION DATA HAS BEEN APPLIED FOR.

TABLE OF CONTENTS

ix

FOREWORD BY DENNIS LOY JOHNSON
AND VALERIE MERIANS

xi

INTRODUCTION BY ALICIA OSTRIKER

xv

FRONTISPIECE: THE WORLD TRADE CENTER
David Lehman

There were, in the immediate aftermath, poems everywhere. Walking around the city you would see them — stuck on light posts and phone stalls, plastered on the shelters at bus stops and the walls of subway stations. In neighborhood newspapers the letters-to-the-editor pages were full of them. Downtown, people scrawled poems in the ash that covered everything. And on the brick walls of police stations and firehouses, behind the mountains of flowers and between photos of the dead, poetry dominated. Eventually, a fire chief actually issued a statement: Thank you for the food and the blankets and the flowers but please — no more poetry.

It put one in mind of Adorno's famous statement: No more poetry in the wake of the Holocaust. And yet, there it was, everywhere. Prose wasn't enough. There was something more to be said that only poetry could say. Everybody, apparently, knew this.

And so, while we heard from distant friends we hadn't heard from in years, all wondering if we'd survived, how we were, how in the world we would persist, we decided we wanted to know the same about poetry, at this remarkable moment in human history, in the poetry capital of the U.S., when there was no question that everything had changed as suddenly as if someone had thrown a switch.

Thus, the poems you find gathered here. We asked poets in and around New York City not for something therapeutic or explicatory or even commemorative; we asked them to simply chime in with work they had done since the event that they felt showed its influence. That's all. The results, we hope readers will find, are nonetheless inherently commemorative of the lasting impact of that terrible, terrible day, but also of something more, and perhaps transcendent.

What's more, we found, in one of the project's many unexpected side benefits, that we'd taken what may be an unprecedented survey of writers working in a certain place at a certain time. And the headcount was high — poets still flock to New York, and the ones already here are not leaving.

As for our main objective, we found that the poets of New York dealt with the events of September 11 with the deepest consideration, with a breadth and scope and vibrancy, that bespoke a kind of psychic fearlessness. And beyond that, of course, there's the notion that the wide-ranging exertion of such imaginative powers constitute in themselves a celebration of the persistence not just of poetry, but of life. The ashes have blown away; the poems have not.

DENNIS LOY JOHNSON
AND VALERIE MERIANS

INTRODUCTION

BY ALICIA OSTRIKER

On the morning of September 11, 2001, my husband and I arrived, tired, at London's Heathrow Airport around dawn, to begin a stay of several months in Cambridge. We made it to our room at Clare Hall, took a nap, went down to the front desk to get a second key, and the World Trade Center Building #1 was on the television, burning, emitting rollers of dark smoke. We and the Brits watched, like everyone else, for days, seeing the same shots over and over, and hearing the same solemn voices.

It was very strange to be so far away. It felt wrong. I buried myself in a cloud of e-mailed poems, and added some, and sent little anthologies to friends. Many of us were doing that. Poetry is important to people in a crisis, as love and intelligence are important. These are survival tools.

Not many of the voices in this book are solemn. Nor do they repeat. Like an explosion, the poems fly out in all directions from an ignited core. No two take the same route to or from Ground Zero, although Stephen Dunn comes close to a definition: "Ground Zero, is it possible to get lower? /... It just takes a little training, to blur / a motive, lie low while planning the terrible," and then asks rhetorically, "who among us doesn't harbor / a grudge or secret?" Forty-five individual responses, all of them authentic and alive. We have our fashions, but by God, we don't do lockstep. We don't follow leaders, we do watch the parking meters. This book is a portrait of the New York temperament, a tangle of cynicism, pride, humor, compassion, and of course confusion. Plus the capacity to absorb hurt and rebound.

My personal taste runs to poetry with attitude. So I like the way David Lehman begins a poem "I never liked the World Trade Center. / When it went up I talked it down." I like Frank Lima's bravura rendition of world news, past, present and future. When Patricia Spears Jones writes "In what cinema are the dreams of mass destruction/so dear as ours," I nod in wry recognition. Ross Martin's little paean to paranoia, "This Poem Will Self Destruct in Sixty Seconds" makes me gasp, and Paul Violi's campy fashion show of warriors in armor is not to be missed.

But there are elegiac poems here too. With "the stadium's sink of glow / damped some hours since," Karl Kirchwey watches "bridge lights looping frailly east" and "far uptown,/ the foursquare garnet constellation / of building lights that blink, solemn, / against a sky empty of planes. /... It is too early and too late." Andrea Carter Brown's "The Old Neighborhood" honors the vanished vendors around the WTC in precise ethnic detail. Miranda Beeson honors a somehow-saved finch. In Tim Suermondt's "Squad 1," a small boy playing fireman decides "it was a rough, dangerous day / on the job / but everyone was saved / from the inferno." In Jean Valentine's "She Would Long," the mother of a girl now ashes yearns to "lie down now, fox in her hole, wild / fox in her hold." And then D. Nurkse describes how memory can go into freeze-frame: "We saw it / and can't stop watching:/... We saw the bodies jump / couldn't break their fall — / now they wait so gracefully/ in midair, holding hands." And then Bill Kushner leaps ecstatic and sobbing into the hairy arms of Walt Whitman calling all the hatemongers to stand back.

How did it feel and what did it mean to be there, at Ground Zero? Or ambling nearby? These poems give some answers. What does it mean to be an American? I think the poems have no answers to that question. In a nation where a president's rating shoots through the ceiling when he starts a war, only two poets in this book talk about retaliation. Eliot Katz frustratedly watches TV "lubricate America's war machine," while Norman Stock's "What I Said" rushes through an unpunctuated sequence of exclamations like "how could this happen and / how could such a thing be and / why why," ultimately segueing into "this is too much to take no one can take a thing like this /...and then I said let's kill them."

I suspect that many poets have mixed feelings about America, not just now but permanently. I do myself. I'm not in love with capitalism, materialism, or militarism. I'm commonly ashamed of USA foreign policy. Of its domestic policies as well. But then again I am proud of my country too. Our culture runs the gamut of highbrow-to-vulgar and beyond. Our creative American energy — and, yes, the money we spend to put that energy to commercial use — is staggering. Our freedom as artists is staggering. Our ability to pull together as a community is fabled. How lucky we are, and we know it. As Rachel Hadas declares, "We mourn and rejoice at once." So many ways of mourning, so many of rejoicing.

The poems in this book are part of what make me proud.

THE WORLD TRADE CENTER

I never liked the World Trade Center.
When it went up I talked it down
As did many other New Yorkers.
The twin towers were ugly monoliths
That lacked the details the ornament the character
Of the Empire State Building and especially
The Chrysler Building, everyone's favorite,
With its scalloped top, so noble.
The World Trade Center was an example of what was wrong
With American architecture,
And it stayed that way for twenty-five years
Until that Friday afternoon in February
When the bomb went off and the buildings became
A great symbol of America, like the Statue
Of Liberty at the end of Hitchcock's *Saboteur.*
My whole attitude toward the World Trade Center
Changed overnight. I began to like the way
It comes into view as you reach Sixth Avenue
From any side street, the way the tops
Of the towers dissolve into the white skies
In the east when you cross the Hudson
Into the city across the George Washington Bridge.

David Lehman, from *Valentine Place*, 1996

POETRY AFTER 9/11

AN ANTHOLOGY OF NEW YORK POETS

Stephen Dunn

GRUDGES

Easy for almost anything to occur.
Even if we've scraped the sky, we can be rubble.
For years those men felt one way, acted another.

Ground zero, is it possible to get lower?
Now we had a new definition of the personal,
knew almost anything could occur.

It just takes a little training, to blur
a motive, lie low while planning the terrible,
get good at acting one way, feeling another.

Yet who among us doesn't harbor
a grudge or secret? So much isn't erasable;
it follows that almost anything can occur,

like men ascending into the democracy of air
without intending to land, the useful veil
of having said one thing, meaning another.

Before you know it something's over.
Suddenly someone's missing at the table.
It's easy (I know it) for anything to occur
when men feel one way, act another.

Aaron Smith

SILENT ROOM

Take a drink of water,
      hold the cup to my lips
    for 8 counts:
      curl my toes, stretch
my fingers, move
      my stomach in and out, in and out.

Twitch my arm,
      twitch my arm, only 5 more times,
   the other,
the same, my ankle,
      blink, blink, blink, blink.

Stare at the lock on the door,
      push it over,
   hold it hard, harder,
push it, 8 counts,
      forget why I'm staring,
         start over, start over.

I haven't done dishes in a week,
      laundry in a month,
         or eaten anything
but McDonald's for lunch
      for as long as I can remember.

I am wearing dirty underwear.
       I am wearing dirty socks.
              I am wearing a dirty T-shirt, and

I can't go to the doctor
             because I know
       I'm dying, I'm dying and
I'm taking
       that damn iron with me tomorrow
             when I leave the apartment.
Its snake-like cord on the floor
       not enough
          to convince me
      it isn't plugged in,
            that everything I am isn't burning.

Miranda Beeson

FLIGHT

An iridescent exhausted finch
found its way to your home
in the aftermath.
Trapped between screen and pane
you palmed him, brought him in,
built him a cage that was not a cage.
A hidden perch for the nights.
An aviary filled with light and seed
for the days.
Where had he come from?
A pet store in the shadow of the towers?
A tiny door unlatched by the blasts?
We pondered dark scenarios.
The survival of this slight speck
of feathered perfection seemed
more important than anything else
we could think of those first few weeks:
more important than the planes,
the slow motion tumble,
the man in his business suit
who fell through the air without
the benefit of wings.

Andrea Carter Brown

THE OLD NEIGHBORHOOD

Where is the man who sold the best jelly donuts and coffee
you sipped raising a pastel blue Acropolis to your lips? Two

brothers who arrived in time for lunch hour with hot and cold
heroes where Liberty dead ends at the Hudson? The courteous

small-boned Egyptian in white robe and crocheted skullcap
in the parking lot behind the Greek Orthodox shrine whose

bananas and dates you could always count on? How about
the tall, slim, dark brown man with dreadlocks cascading

to his waist who grilled Hebrew National franks to perfection
and knew just the right amount of mustard each knish wanted?

The cinnamon-skinned woman for whose roti people lined up
halfway down Church, the falafel cousins who remembered

how much hot pepper you preferred? Don't forget the farmers
who schlepped up from Cape May twice each week at dawn

to bring us whatever was in season at its peak: last August,
blueberries and white peaches. What about the lanky fellow

who sold green and red and yellow bears and fish and snakes
in plastic sandwich bags with twist ties; his friend, a block

away, who scooped still warm nuts from a silver cauldron
into palm-sized wax paper sacks he twisted at the corners

to close? The couple outside the post office with their neatly
laid out Golden Books, the shy Senegalese with briefcases

of watches except in December when they sold Christmas
trees? The Mr. Softee who parked every evening rush hour

by the cemetery to revive the homeward hurrying crowd?
I know none of their names, but I can see their faces clear

as I still see everything from that day as I ride away from
the place we once shared. Where are they now? And how?

Andrea Carter Brown

ASH WEDNESDAY, 2002

On this day, give or take a week or two over
forty years ago, a girl vowed to give up fighting
with her father for forty days and nights. Did
she last? She doesn't remember. Probably not.
Every day is an anniversary of sorts. This Ash
Wednesday, for example, will become, the day
she found, walking down a block she's sure she's
never walked before in the city where she's lived
most of those forty years, a fire house standing
between two school playgrounds. The top pane
of its one window is covered by a photograph
of a man cradling a Dalmatian, both crouched
before Seagrave Engine 44. Handsome as the day
is firefighter Mike Lyons. Filling the lower pane,

a hot pink oak tag poster with black magic marker
"It's a girl!", announcing the safe arrival of Mary
Michael, his daughter, I couldn't be more sure,
7 pounds, 10 ounces, on November 2nd, one day
shy of my birthday, the second since Dad died
on 10/4, the first since 9/11. As I stand there,
the newly fatherless considering the newborn
who will never know hers, the engine returns
from a call, polished bright but clearly not new,
pausing before it eases through the narrow portal
to shoo the kids clustered outside. Then the door
closes as the crew scrambles down, separating
those who knew Mike Lyons from those who
wish we had, their grief from the burden of ours.

Bill Kushner

FRIENDS

Everyone says he's depressed
but what does that mean? Dean
always waits & waits but he waits
what for? isn't life too short?
Lewis is cautious at first, but then
quick to love. Ruth fell down
& broke her crown, but now, in
a sling, she's home. Richard just
got back from the world & what
he says it's from awful to okay. Too
soon, school begins, & too soon
the autumn. Why I always get so
sad when I see the leaves turning
falling, in a flame. Lillian, she
goes on buses that goes to see them
but I never can. Charlotte? she
remains unheard from, is that Piaf
singing? she who regrets nothing, oh
Don, dear Don, out walking, when
last seen, in the rain. A call from
Karin, Bob's birthday, & a week
or so later, it's Paul's, & he's turning
thirty, of all peoples, turning thirty
come weep, let's dance. Paul & Justin
went down to the site to help dig
day after it happened, good boys
good men. Faye? still painting away
still searching for beauty where where-

ever it's hiding, come out, let's play.
Lilla's still back & forth, the house
New York, the house. I think she's
still grieving, you can grieve a long
time, every thing takes a long time
no? Rose? is forever aglow, no
matter the what, but that's her, that's
our Rose.

Bill Kushner

CIVILIZATION

You talk to me, I listen. I
talk to you, you listen. Is
this like civilization or
what? We watch our hands,
fingers knotting, twisting, for
something hidden. "Everything
you say" you say with a grin
"probably makes perfect sense
in some other world." We,
even in this silence, listen,
but whatever for? but still
we cock our heads so, what
a great conversation we are al-
most having. An elderly Chinese
man looks at us curiously, his
parched old wrinkled face stares,
unblinking, inscrutable, as if
across some strange vast distance,
but only I seem to notice him,
you are far away. I wonder
what would happen if I held
out my arms, and if I took him
in them, his thin frail foreign
body, and simply held him and
our two hearts together, would
that be unheard of? would
it upset the balance of the world

and tip it over? He continues
his steady gaze as you suddenly
stand. "You coming or staying?"
I don't say anything, and you
walk away, but lumbering slowly
as is your way, as if a fierce wind
you keep punching against it
it keeps punching you back.

Bill Kushner

IN THE HAIRY ARMS OF WHITMAN

I am walking reading Walt Whitman's Leaves of Grass & I
    stop in traffic look around
I am Whitman dying thinking of a good last poem
I am Whitman on death's bed sobbing for Lincoln for
    Kennedy for King I am
Whitman scattering lilacs sobbing I am at once myself & Whitman
    we 2 ghosts
I am my mother Fannie my father Max as we ghosts step
    immigrants on America's shores
I am Whitman sobbing for us the tired the poor the wretched refuse
    I am
Whitman sobbing for all victims of discrimination regardless of race
    sex age color creed
I am Whitman sobbing for Matthew Shephard for Mahatma Gandhi for
    Joan of Arc
                O so many martyrs
                September 11th
I am walking beside you Whitman we stop for a moment
On the corner of 14th where we wait for a light light to hit us & change
& stroking your white beard as you look at me & I stroking too
    this is for forever
Where & when forever ends I slurp a good hot soup with Whitman
In a good hot soup kitchen a bunch of us hairy bums we are
But a bunch of us slurping hairy bums & Whitman & I
Whitman walking with a hardon in the heart of gay Chelsea I am
Whitman digging at the site of the World Trade Center
O as all the buildings do explode around about us

I am angry poet Whitman flying at the fragments flying
     papers ash flesh
Whitman screaming into air for only Whitman he shall
     put us together
Whitman screaming freedom Whitman long-haired hippie
     crying Love
Love love I say to you I am all in a moment
I am gorgeous Whitman in drag I am Whitman the solemn President
In the White House calling all the armies Come back
Come back! calling all the hatemongers Stand back Stand back
O hear me! hear me! we are all leaves of grass
I am end of the day I am all that remains of you O Walt Whitman at
The end of the day & I naked & Whitman naked & I in
     Whitman's hairy arms
& all we yes in his dreamy hairy arms O the dreamy hairy arms
     of Whitman
O see Whitman as he dreams he is restless stirring O as he Whitman
     dreams

Star Black

SKYSCRAPERS

Night's glass towers, Rapunzel'd by the sun,
still stand at attention when the work's all done
like dragon dogs guarding the Mahayana heavens, or sentries
at the outpost, leaning, nodding. Solariums

of labor, they're useless to the moon, pitched
punctuation without any words. Harbors of security
to paper-clipping functions now rest in darkness
as mute gongs in an infinite forest,

elevators and alarms shut-eyed in silence,
thirteenth floors snuffed. They seem, to tiny slumberers
doorsteps from their lobby, friendly giants

who nuzzle dreams in tiny apartments, as if, tired
from standing, they roll back, as a shoulder onto a pillow,
to let a neighbor know the nightmare's over.

Star Black

ASYLUM

In the unmannered madhouse
of the typical mind,
its swinish discontents
and skeetering emotions,

upon its disheveled doss
and rabbly bedspread,
two firebugs
buzz tête-à-tête.

They connect and disconnect
through the dogtooth days.
Pray for them.
They are small and

cannot live inside long.
Open a window.

Shelley Stenhouse

CIRCLING

At night the fighter planes circle
and I look at the yellowed corner of my ceiling
where the dead mosquito hangs
and remember last summer's fear of disease -
bearing bugs, the whoosh of the mosquito trucks,
and my favorite Post headline LET US SPRAY.
Lately I'm afraid of all sounds and the lack of sounds.
News voices, *guarding reactors* — my daughter
hates the news, why is she watching?
And where have the backyard birds gone?
The *yo babay mo-fo boom chicka* Jersey cars
don't blast around my block trying to park.
We'll never go back. It's so strange to be caught
in history, to be making history after just making loads
of unused imaginary money, men in blue jackets shouted,
traded, and it's gone and it's okay but I don't want to die.
I hope God is circling up there with those planes.
Patti was a good person and she died.
God is probably passed out somewhere warm and dark,
still sleeping off his whole world, seven day binge
and it's just us, warring unhinged teenagers
trashing this big beautiful park.

Hal Sirowitz

SLOWING DOWN FOR DEATH

My father detested the drivers who slowed down
whenever there was an accident in the opposite lane,
so they could take a peek. They were making
his trip home take longer. He said they were
like vultures, but instead of getting a meal
out of it they only saw, if they were lucky,
a few dead bodies. He didn't think
death was so interesting. He knew
it was human nature to want to look,
to feel relieved that it wasn't you
looking like a lifeless doll, but he felt
it was more respectful not to look —
to give the dead a little privacy.
He was sure if it was worth looking at
it'd be on the TV by the time we got home.

Hal Sirowitz

COOKIES FOR PEACE

Father said if I gave the boy who was teasing me
a bloody nose he'd stop. Mother didn't think
it was good advice. She said I wouldn't
get far in life if I tried to punch everyone
who bothered me. She wanted my father to think
of a better solution. He didn't have any.
He said if we didn't like his advice
we should ask someone else. She said
she'd continue to ask father, because there was
always some hope he'd change. She knows
one day the boy will change too, feel badly
about teasing me & wish he was nicer.
She could speed along his transformation
by giving me cookies to give to him.
The next day he teased me like he always did.
But I felt I got revenge by eating his cookies.

Carter Ratcliff

SO GALLANTLY STREAMING: TO THE POET

Of all your poems,
I am the favorite, but not
your favorite.

You are bored with me, so bored
that you left me out of your *Selected Poems*.

I had become your name,
syllables meaning only you,
so all you could mean was me,
whose meaning had now been chiseled

deep into the ramparts of the stone that fortifies
the day our language, which is our nation,

was invented. Forget those petrified depths.

This is what my exclusion tells me,
tells us all, as we contrive to keep our heads
above the water which not only laves us.

It provides us
with the only believable surfaces
on which to write anything at all,
for only surfaces are believable,
for they are all in all

that flows into the future,
the current that keeps us
and our names alive.

Because I had become your name,
leaving me out of your *Selected Poems*
was your bid for namelessness — an ironic bid,
like a fly's bid for amber,

for only the false hope of being nameless
reminds you to be yourself, always yourself because
never unbuoyed by the hope that in reciting me,

your admirers are not simply wearing out your name,
they are truly breathing, as only they can do,
for that is what we do

in our nation, breathe
for ourselves, sunk but still swimming
in the air that still holds us all in common.

Eliot Katz

WHEN THE SKYLINE CRUMBLES

Was sitting Astoria kitchen chair about to vote mayoral primary,
then would've hopped subway to work Soho's Spring Street —
turned TV on for quick election check when CNN switched
    to picture of World Trade Center #1
with surreal gaping hole blowing dark smoke out a new mouth.
Witnesses still in shock were describing a plane flying
    directly into the building's side
when a second plane suddenly crashed Twin Tower 2
and orange flames & monstrous dust rolls began replacing
    the city's world renowned skyline.
Soon the big city's tallest buildings crumbled, one at a time —
with 50,000 individual heartbeats working in Twin Bodies,
    it was clear this horror going to be planetfelt.

I stared stunned at TV another half hour, called Vivian working
    Canadian summer forest job to assure I was physically okay
& mourn together, then wandered my Queens neighborhood —
almost everyone walking mouths open silent, eyes unblinking,
two women & two men on 31st Street cried into cell phones,
    trying reach loved ones working the WTC,
a mover moaned Age Old prophecy to his buddy loading the van:
    "The world has changed, bro."

Wednesday I subway'd into Manhattan looking to volunteer
    with bad back,
only found location to leave a donation check, all other slots
    remarkably filled for the moment —
also wanted to sense the air fellow Applers were breathing,

smoke that torched bodies now tangibly coating tongue &
    nostrils, dust burning all 3 eyes —
7th Ave above 14th St almost empty rush hour so our dead
    could be counted, a clear road to the next realm,
perhaps a friend's friend miraculously uncovered alive,
    given space to speed St. Vincent's Emergency Room.

Thursday I sat half hour Union Square with a Tibetan group
    meditating for peace
as mainstream TV helped lubricate America's war machine
    hosting Flat Earth hawks urging 80% toward retaliation
against Bin Laden or any country harboring Bin Laden's cells —
even as academic analysts noted moments before those cells
    now spread to 30 countries including US.
Fox News had hosted a discussion between the far right
    & further right —
Newt Gingrich: the terrorists should be found & crushed —
Jeanne Kirkpatrick: we already know who they are, why wait —
a procession of military experts advocating carpet bombs & napalm.

On Friday night, 3000 New Yorkers, mostly young,
    candlelit Union Square
to mourn the victims & stand for peace with signs like:
    "War is Not the Answer" &
"Honor the Dead; Break the Cycle of Violence" —
CBS–TV covered the event as another cute show of
    the city's spirit of togetherness

sandwiched between two dozen stories of a flag–waving public
    meat–hungry to support Bush Jr's rush to war.

After years of U.S. missiles flying into outward shores,
a decade after 100,000 Iraqis cruise missile'd to death
    under Father George
The war has now come home, where it's apparent to all
    what a senseless random murderer
    is the one–eyed giant Terror
how it eats its innocent victims screaming alive, feet flailing
how it breaks the strongest of backs, rips flesh wide open
how it tosses arms East, legs South, skull & genitals
    North & West
how it forces hardened athletes to dive head first 99 floors
    to a concrete death softer than its iron teeth
how it leaves no paperwork behind to comfort the living
how it answers pleading mothers & weeping babes
    with a knife to the belly, glass shards to throat
how it burns a skyline of fresh bones to fragile white ash

Now, we walk memory's long marathon to honor our 5,000 dead
now we watch a million New Yorkers work courageously
    to meet the initial test
daily tasks small to heroic, delivering socks, pulling two–ton girders
    off fallen firefighters atop creaky broken floors
ignoring fear everpresent, unknown particles filling the air —
now we see whether Americans can meet the next human challenge:

Protect the innocent & reject Terror in all its disguises,
    even strutting on TV in our own leaders' garb?
Or merely act a mirror of its latest highrise profile?
The sometimes bitter juices of justice, law, human rights, & peace?
Or shot after shot of eternal bloodthirst?

Eliot Katz

THE WEATHER SEEMS DIFFERENT

It is snowing in Athens tonight & Apollo with ice in his beard
          is having a difficult time singing
About six twin engine miniplanes have crashed coast to coast
          in empty fields & a Bank of America building
My love, you know that death is both a separation
          and a permanent glue
You know that I am the son of a patient duct tape expert
          and the daughter of a wine never allowed to age
Love, we are all things to each, we are needy in just the ways
          each other needs but doesn't yet comprehend
In the open fields of Somalia there are civilians running circles
          freaked out shivering they might be next
From a satellite 10,000 miles above earth, like an empty chair
          with telescope
a disembodied human eye stares at us & stares at Columbia
          he is looking below the oceans for new caves
He is looking for people who are not yet in favor of empty chairs
          placing nuclear-tipped dynamite in empty caves
The danger is real, one can feel it in the air
          even if unsure from which directions it is borne
We are all getting older, we have realized this year it's time
          to get serious about ducking death's temporary wings
Time to get our 10-dimensional affairs in order, between your
          big toe and its chipped nail
there is a fire-breathing vulture just waiting for the dimensional wall
          to collapse even for a millisecond
History repeats itself but sometimes as a young student pilot
          unsure how to create an effective farce

My dear, the vulture escaped for my 45th birthday last night
      it was in our bedroom pecking below the sheets
It has eaten us alive and regurgitated us back into this world —
      time will tell whether we are healthier than before

Jean Valentine

IN THE BURNING AIR

In the burning air
nothing.

But on the ground
      Let the sadness be
a woman and her spoon,
a wooden spoon,
and her chest, the broken
bowl.

Jean Valentine

SHE WOULD LONG

She would long
to dig herself into the graveyard, her only
daughter's ashes
in her nose   in her mouth   her only daughter's
makeshift ashes
nothing
lying
in the hole in her chest

But her eye would still see
up   into   the graveyard above her, still see
the feet, the flowers

Yes her daughter will be an orchard
Yes the orchard will be a forest

— Let her lie down now, fox in her hole, wild
fox in her hold.

Scott Hightower

TONTINE

May 23, 1864

At Pemigewasset House
Pierce and Hawthorne took adjoining rooms and slept
with the connecting
door ajar. A dog's
bark stirred the ex-President from his
sleep, but — "in the twinkling of
an eye" — not the other weary traveler.
Sumner wrote to Longfellow,
"One by one,
almost in twos, they seem to go."

Vicki Hudspith

NODDING CRANES

No one wants to look at my disaster
It has become a construction site
A reconstructive epicenter of trucks

And nodding cranes
Starving ballerinas
Dipping into molten lava

At night it is flooded with unyielding white light
Bouncing off random windows.
A bathing suit dressing room. A reaper.

My disaster is receding
It encompasses less and less of every block
Fewer streets know it each day

My disaster is still a disaster
But autumn is faithful and refuses winter
Its place

I am protective of my disaster, do not want to let it go
Instead, I would like to embrace it
As it once embodied my horror

And if all the pieces are swept away
How will I measure
What I know

Distraction is a comfort to my disaster
Welcomed with the exhilaration of new information
A baby sleeps in a stroller

Your brain knows my disaster
As a science fiction of vaporizing steel and daily habits
As well as the plans I have to rebuild my disaster

Norman Stock

WHAT I SAID

after the terror I
went home and cried and
said how could this happen and
how could such a thing be and
why why I mean how could
anything so horrible and how could
anyone do such a thing to us and what
will happen next and how can we live now
it's impossible to understand it's impossible
to do anything after this and what will any of us do now and how will we live
    and how can we expect to go on after this
I said and I said this is too much to take no one can take a thing like this
after the terror yes and then I said let's kill them

Colette Inez

SEPTEMBER MORNING

decreed a light
whose beauty
stared the passengers down
like Shiva wearing a garland
of serpents and skulls.
Soon the queen of fire
and the king of ashes danced.
Towers fell.
From a pocket of air under stone,
imagined voices seeped out
like water from a fissure
in the earth.
Now they ask for nothing
in a world that waits for them
if we invent it —
mysterious like houses
they once entered, keyholes
squeezing in the light,
every room abundant.

Colette Inez

THE SKEPTIC

I am the free-thinker who reads Voltaire.
   A photograph of Karl Marx adorns my piano.
I quote from Robert Ingersoll's "Why I Am an Agnostic."
   "I doubt therefore I am" never said by Pascal,
yet I am and I doubt any interpretation
   of god that doesn't also describe him as a symbolic
tribal father hurling biblical rancor at the nations.
   I doubt his alleged only son as anything more than a
dissident perched in fictive heaven
   among angels who sometimes fly down to earth to keep drunks
and debtors from jumping into rivers.
   I doubt celestial virgins will visit the men who ate pizza
in Florida, shopping smart at discount stores.
   Consigned to the zero of null, they are specks of ash
alongside those they killed in the name of their divinity.
I want to put an extra "O" between G O and D, I'll pray
to that: love, friends, music, books, reason and beauty.

David Trinidad

ADAM AND EVE ON THE HOLLYWOOD
TREAD MILL

Adam and Eve on the Hollywood treadmill
     out of sync with the pedestrians behind them

a process shot of a New Haven sidewalk
     The Evildoers emerge from the Shubert Theater

and stroll, gloating, towards the Taft Hotel
     (Think Bonnie stroking Clyde's gun on a street corner

Think Faye Dunaway's "rag-doll dance of death"*
     as gun blasts keep her body in motion)

"What a Heav'nly day," says Eve, envisioning a dark victory
     Addison likens the out-of-town opening to D-Day

The Allied invasion (known as Operation Overlord)
     of the European continent through Normandy in WWII

Casualties: 637,000 soldiers were killed, wounded
     or captured during the campaign, June 6-Aug. 29, 1944

a war reference that would have seemed outdated
     a mere month ago, pre-WTC

Note sign behind Addison and Eve:
     U.S. ARMY RECRUITING SERVICE

The Agents of Evil emerge from an elevator
    on the shadow-slit fifth floor of the Taft Hotel

Eve: "It'll be a night to remember."
    (Think Titanic: British luxury passenger liner

that sank on the night of Apr. 14-15, 1912
    after crashing into an iceberg

in the North Atlantic south of Newfoundland
    More than 1,500 lives were lost

Think Kate Winslet in a diaphanous evening gown
    up to her waist in freezing water

apparently immune to hypothermia
    being rescued by teen idol Leonardo DiCaprio

Think inexplicable pop phenomenon Celine Dion
    warbling "My Heart Will Go On" [and on and on])

In the corridor they pass a black wall phone, a fire hose
    (Think Carrie's telekinetic revenge at the prom

her fire hose uncoiling like a cobra
    blasting all those nasty kids

'l'he death toll staggering: teachers, administrators,
    the entire graduating class [save Sue Snell])

Eve a Morticia-like bride in black: coat, hat, veil pulled back
    no need "to shroud her face / And the want graven there"**

Everything she's ever wanted within her grasp
    But first a nice long nap

*Pauline Kael
**Christina Rossetti, "Bride Song"

"Adam and Eve on the Hollywood Treadmill" is an excerpt from Phoebe 2002: An
Essay in Verse, a collaboration with Jeffery Conway and Lynn Crosbie. Phoebe 2002
is a mock-epic based on the 1950 movie All About Eve.—D.T.

Hugh Seidman

NEW YORK

I read over my lines
(terrible hubris,
terrible debris).

I have been too soft:
car skid in the rain,
black eye over a woman,
105 fever of pneumonia.

I confess that my parents
suffered heart attack,
dementia, stroke.

Sometimes I had anger,
whatever it meant.

Sometimes I wept,
as if in spite of myself.

(Brown, thick smoke
against dusk turquoise.)

I had entered
fluorescent cubicles.

I had crossed tunnels
under tons of water,
under the tomb
that is cosmos.

I had poured coffee,
tasted bread,
watched TV
blaring stocks, war.

(The Airbus 300
has struck Belle Harbor.)

Fear is what I lacked
(terrible motion,
terrible implode),
down to the soles,
the involuntary wail
that changes soul.

Each atom of the body
from the start of the stars.

One molecule at least, say,
of Caesar's breath.

Charlie Smith

RELIGIOUS ART

Certain precautions, obstacles
set against vandals — the stretch
of highway, for example, outside Nichols, New Mexico,
loneliness like a family art,
a man's idea of himself
pinned down in the Holy Land, strings of peppers
drying on a porch.

I press hard with my feet
against the earth and
call this fighting back. All yesterday
I walked around counting birds.
Trees, a spray of pebbles in the forecourt,
a dip the wind took about six

maintain the posts assigned, repel boarders.

The peculiar emptiness
in the mown hayfield this afternoon
we stood staring into — as a precaution —
the clefts and shadowy declines containing
our deepest interests, the grass shining and then going dull against
the fading light, these were protection enough.

Frank Lima

GOOD MORNING AMERICA

The United States of America rose at dawn this morning after a restless
Night and many horrent dreams, still courting freedom, like the author of
Brightness. Will we never sleep again, even though the blood of the dead
Hangs in space on the other side of the world on the dried beard of that
Unkempt gyrovague. Freedom is the dramatic dislocation of evil.

Little is recorded or remembered about the life of the stars on our flag.
At the time the rent was reasonable, there was an abundance of space,
And no demons to fear; we had left them behind in Europe to their own
Means, continuing their tradition of unhappiness in the name of some god
When pronounced correctly, sounded like a Spanish cough syrup from

The Renaissance. This god's voice was originally a thousand lemons and
Saffron and its truth was a mild day in the desert. Camels had not
Discovered the innocence of desert plums or veiled women with fragrant
Wisdom forbidden to enjoy the touch of the sun's location. Yet, their
Mistreatment of women is not a divine law, and most of what is

Contained in manufactured memory is not legal, just talk. Sand and
Dryness is no environment for slender arms and kisses. The soul is not a
Fragment falling from the trinity of a window. Love purifies but does not
Systemize dogma for it is not a true behavior of the heart: It is vision at
The end of living. The stars on the flag have become the casualties of

Our open society. In a single, envious denouncement from the Middle
Ages our blue skies' became grey and acrid yellow like their speeches to
The deities in the desert. This philosophical hysteria is a western cloud
Carried across the earth by eagles made of crusty bread for the men
And women of the sun. The wallpaper on the World Trade Center

Is a metaphoric label on a religious bottle of malignancy at sea with a
Note that reads, "This is freedom in the ocean of sandy hatred from the
Cloudy eyes and ogee lips of our God." The Dead Sea Scrolls are no
Longer the tenants of caves. There is a road that leads to the West
Covered with the fluid of diamonds. This road leads to a fixed point

Among the stars where the Bible and the Koran pick one another's
Feathers at the end of Each day counting the number of disbelievers in
The Grains of sand. My children and my wife are the spots of glitter in
The sand on sunny days or rainy days, when freedom conducts services
For the lost footprints and the future of dreaming.

Tony Towle

IMMATERIAL NOCTURNES:
HUDSON AND WORTH

As the car alarms disconcertingly
respond to each other's pitch
I look down the former Anthony Street,
a former Anthony myself, where the moon
is full on the ears of Leon the donkey and
the hibiscus tree remains untamed
but picturesque and leaning a little forward
as if to peek out between the curtains to the asphalt below
where a diagram of the 1943 Battle of Kursk has been laid out
in myriad notations of red and orange.
Notice the arrows near the parking lot, where
Rossokovsky's T-34's will penetrate the German salient.
At dawn instructors will utilize jackhammers
to simulate the voracious clamor of battle
and trace the route of the attack. We will lie sleepless
in our bunkers until the lesson is complete.

Tony Towle

PROSPECTS

I would like to live long enough to see the State Quarters Program
clink to a successful conclusion, twelve dollars and fifty cents
of wealth and history fulfilled in cardboard circles,
however now the text will take a different direction,
for as Kentucky was about to embody the twenty-five-cents
needed for its second admission to the Union, the imps of haphazard historicity
subjected the skyline to the whims of religious psychopaths;
and before that I had never purchased an American flag —
since I always knew where I *was* and, when abroad,
at least in England, the natives always knew where I was *from* —
but in October I bought two; from immigrants making a tenuous living,
appropriately, from Africa and Asia, respectively
and on Wall Street, no less.

Tony Towle

DIPTYCH

Cactus poachers work quickly
and we cactuses know it;
keeping our spines
sticking straight out all night
is an effort well worth it
when we hear a curse and feel a drop of blood;
then our "eyes" twinkle in the depth of our
anthropomorphized pulp
on the giant land mass veiled here and there
by these dabs of metamorphosis,
until I can imagine myself in that space,
planted before a background of tropical dots,
or until I imagine myself in *that* space, falling
through the exploded event
of burnt electricity and pulverized death.
And so I will tell you about life on my planet
since I will get tired of just standing here:
our oxygen needs are simple, but wit, laughter
and ambiguity are made to carry gloom,
lamentation and humorlessness on their shoulders.

Molly Peacock

THE LAND OF THE SHÍ

The Land of the Shí
is the same land we inhabit only
the heart beats more insistently.
All green is Green, you'd say,
everything gray is itself, only more Gray.
You can stand in the place you're standing in
and enter the Land of the Shí.
Even the rain which rains on Avenue A
in the Land of the Shí rains silkier
and you, parched in New York City,
become more deeply quenched.
The ear of a pug who waits at the light
is silkier and more pugly.
Money is exactly the same rate,

except that every dollar has individual weight,
and a New York City kiss
in the Land of the Shí is palpable as sculpted flesh.
It is the beautiful place we yearned for as boys and girls,
the Land of Faery one needs only mental transport for.
Oh brown institutional housing of the He,
vanish beneath, vanish beneath
as detritus into running water. . . .
That pug in his red rainboots at the corner
now breathes free through two little nostrils cleared
in the Land of Faery. The dry cleaners is still
on the corner across from the 24-hr Deli,

and a lost thought appears for a moment
as a tender face on a penny.

The Land of the Shi is another name for the world underneath the Celtic faery
mounds—a parallel, alternate world where one can take refuge after a catastrophe.
—M.P.

Philip Schultz

FREE MERCY

The woman beside me on the Jitney weeps
into a cell phone, "You're leaving me!"
Every seat is taken, it's late and I'm tired
so I rehearse objections as she cries, "Billy!
You love the way I swim! You love my eyes!"
I try a childhood distraction trick: my dog
Rusty runs away, it's my birthday and beautiful
Miss Crittenden, my first grade teacher, is leaving
to get married... "Hear that?" the woman cries,
ripping a magazine. "It's my heart!" My father
dies bankrupt and I don't go to college... "That time
you saw the cuts on my wrist and asked if I'd do *that*
over you and I said no? I *was* lying." I stutter, lisp,
apologize too much... "I'm coming back to an empty house?"
My number is called, I'm going to Vietnam... "Billy, please,
a little mercy..."

Last Sunday my son got tired of skating so we walked
around the cemetery by the pond and stopped to read
a poem named "Free Mercy" inscribed on a stone in 1688,
about a boy who died at sea "innocent and happy" and
I wondered if it meant one shouldn't have to pay for it,
and we stood there, my wife, son, the baby and me, each
a tiny piece of free luck, and the kids skating behind us,
laughing, as if Miss Crittenden would never leave them.

Sharon Kraus

(WE) PROMENADE

The comfort of the former. He's running
up and down your once, its cobblestones

and brocaded iron. Others here, holding cameras and
hands – then to fend off the past of the future. The writer
is a harsh critic and herself somewhat fends off the present which was

before and around, in the shape of a light beam in the shape of a
stele in the shape of an absence in the shape of one hundred ten
storeys in the shape of their particles in the shape of their representation in
the shape of the live atoms shaking off heat in the shape of light which one

might not notice – I picked him up and said
                          Look, here's something Important and
he did not understand and inclined his shoulders and torso toward
Then I knew it was the mother taking

warmth of the child and took a picture "His Promenading"
(his back to the lens to his
mother's gaze) (she is a monolith) (he will need to crumble it to see her)

arms for balance like wings   Now he's fallen and you run to

Tell him it will be okay.   In the light of.   Just say it.

Douglas Goetsch

WHAT KEEPS ANIMALS SANE?

Curled here, my cat is riding this couch
the way the men and women of Star Trek
rode the Enterprise, watching galaxies approach.
If I were my cat I think I'd kill myself —
waking and dozing all day like a drunk
without even a thought for where his mother is.
The most frequently reported hallucination
under *Delirium Tremens:* spiders crawling all over.
That's beer, not heroin. We forget
household vices can be that worldly serious,
just as we forget how foreign America really is,
so strange and national. We drive by
the Seven-Eleven and think of nothing.
I don't know where my mother is.
Probably in a foreign land called Virginia.
I assume they're treating her poorly
or indifferently. A woman
overweight, wearing sweatpants.
In the last years I knew her she drove
a stick shift. She wasn't good at it,
but it was what she liked now.
My cat meows more since the death
of the other cat, who he hated,
just as we in New York City
sometimes get attached to droning alarms,
which we hate, then miss.

Anne-Marie Levine

FOUR NOVEMBER 9THS

My family expected I would be born on Armistice Day,
November 11, and that would be one thing,
that would have been something to joke about
in those days. But I came into being two days earlier,
on November 9, in the evening, and that was another thing,
it was not a joke, and it was evidently not a thing
to be remembered or told,
because I was not made aware of the coincidence
of my birthday until several months before my 50th birthday,
which coincided with, and was commemorated and announced as,
the 50th anniversary of Kristallnacht.
So there I was, and even more than that here I am,
quite surprised, not to mention still unprepared,
and quite unable to avoid thinking about both at once.
The reminders since then have been constant and grim.
Coincidence: the visible traces of invisible principles.

And now my friend Gottfried Wagner,
who since the day he discovered the date
has never forgotten my birthday,
has informed me that there are four November 9ths
in history, that it is a very big day in the history of Germany
in this century. There is even a book written,
it is called *The Four November 9ths*.
I can't read the book, it is written in German,
but I have done some research, and as far as I can tell

The first November 9 was 1918;
it was a revolution in which the Kaiser abdicated,
which culminated in the Proclamation of the Republic in Berlin
on November 9. The above-mentioned Armistice
between the Allies and Germany
followed on the 11th.

The second November 9 was 1923;
it was Hitler's abortive "Beer Hall Putsch"
against the Bavarian government in Munich.
Hitler, who was at first imprisoned, eventually emerged
as the undisputed leader of the radical right.

The third November 9 was, as you know, My November 9th,
Kristallnacht.

And on Nov. 9, 1989, the Berlin Wall came down.

So there you are and here we are, on my birthday,
and all of this is to say what Gertrude Stein has already said,
what can I teach you about history — history teaches.

It is not a simple matter, the birthday, or the telling.

Nancy Mercado

GOING TO WORK

On their daily trips
Commuters shed tears now
Use American flags
Like veiled women
To hide their sorrows
Rush to buy throwaway cameras
To capture your twin ghosts

Frantically I too
Purchase your memory
On post cards & coffee mugs
In New York City souvenir shops
Afraid I'll forget your façade
Forget my hallowed Sunday
Morning Path Train rides
My subway travels through
The center of your belly
Day after day

Afraid I'll forget your powers
To transform helicopters
Into ladybugs gliding in the air
To turn New York City
Into a breathing map
To display the curvature
Of our world

Ross Martin

THIS MESSAGE WILL SELF-DESTRUCT IN SIXTY SECONDS

If I've done this right
you're leaning up against
a granite wall at the abandoned
warehouse wherethefuckknowswhere
wearing inappropriate shoes and a sweat-
soaked wife-beater your hair
looks fine stop worrying the bullet
hole in your shoulder is just cosmetic
you've caught your breath by now
haven't you forgotten about being
so hungry (sorry to remind you) now
that you're hungry again chew
the Bubblicious we stuck in
your pocket (but quietly!) and listen
carefully to what I'm about to say:

There's a microchip in you somewhere
but we don't know where it is
there's something evil in you but
we don't know where there's something
benignly homosexual in you but we don't
know where and hopefully we will come
to find there's something more than vaguely
heroic in you but we don't know when
what we're saying is there's a whole new
you in you so hurry up before it's too late
man listen to me I'm telling it to you
like it is it's your only chance they are

coming man they're right behind you
they are right on your freakin' tail.
Go.

Philip Fried

EARLY, LATE

When the roofs of cars are themselves a fiery
road of spectral highlights and drivers
stick shadows on the empty street —
that early, the self might overflowing

meet itself coming the other way,
as once in a garden or mirror, but now
in the memory of a city of windows
each wider than its narrow house,

the inner life open for inspection —
upright comfort, sin swept away —
a shipshape city properly tied
with long and orderly lengths of water.

Somewhere in that city, but where
I could never be sure, is a miniature
of the city, reproducing every
bridge, canal house, and canal.

It has a life of its own, it lives
brief days and nights, twilights, dawns,
quicker than normal, nanoseconds
for seconds, and so it is older, older.

Meters for millimeters, a flying
object would shadow Regulierstraat

unidentified and a smaller you
cringing would encounter your own

finger, that's why it's better not
to meet oneself coming from another
dimension, to say, I could not find
the miniature and there is no doubling

of every thing, the wind blows
uniquely in its wayward way,
all the stick men enter their fiery
cars and drive them into the day.

Karl Kirchwey

NOCTURNE, MORNINGSIDE HEIGHTS

Not expunged,
not by the city's ambient light,
the three stars of Orion's belt
cinched tight as a Yankee pitcher's blouse,
the stadium's sink of glow
damped some hours since,
the thread (I did not say threat)
of bridge lights looping frailly east
toward the dawn five hours away,
the muezzein's call
across the green bronze cornices of Harlem
(no, no, the sun will not have seen
anything greater) and, far uptown,
the foursquare garnet constellation
of building lights that blink, solemn,
against a sky empty of planes,
no sob of passage overhead.
The city lies all unprostrated.
It is too early and too late.

Eileen Myles

FLOWERS

Flowers
are out
all over
New York.
Every deli
tonight is
lit with
mad daffodils
jonquils
baby's
breath
eucalyptus
pussy willow
blasts of
cox comb
roses,
irises. It's
Spring. I pick
pink gerber
daisies. I pick
two then begin
veering off
into hotter
pink-orange
flowers
then white,
no red.

The mix is
a mess. I
throw back
the difference
& slip in another
daisy — fully
pink then
another one. A big
pink group —
surefire same-
ness is good.
It's strong.
In the car
they look yellow
you said.
No pink.
Really? I'm
freaking out.
We turn on
the light.
You won.
They're pretty.
Later we're
parked at
another
brightly-lit store.
Same spring.
Hundreds

of flowers
outside as
the world
continues
its impossible
turning. We
miss you.

Lewis Warsh

BEFORE I WAS BORN

There is a moment of separation
between two things, & one of them is living.
A moth is living, is still alive.
And all this is happening on the other side
       of the river.

Life is multiple, I have multiple selves, a past.
And different languages are spoken in office
       buildings & tents.
Equipment is arranged along a shoreline.
The lights in the buildings go out, one at a time.

The man on the subway platform is playing the accordion.
I make a fist, then relax, my fingers are trembling.
Bulbs burn out on an exit sign, the color of beef
       at a lunch counter.
A woman on the subway reading War and Peace

asks me to follow her but I get lost in the crowd.
To obey with your eyes closed is the beginning of panic.
Nothing I do can impede the flow.
My oldest friend bursts into tears on the street.

If I could only have one thought at a time
& remember that there are others who think
       the same way
& elsewhere — a man is preparing food for his child.
And elsewhere, a woman folds her skirt
       over the back of a chair.

Take a page out of your own book & remember
       the river beneath the bridge.
We pass over the Alps in a train in the middle of night.
My arms are forgotten in the motion of the train
       moving, word by word.

Kimiko Hahn

MORTAL REMAINS

Who could have guessed, attention glued
to John Travolta hustling his ass off
in polyester and sweat
inside the 2001 Space Odyssey —
that that image of prime sexuality
from the era when even I turned the heads —
at least those of hard hats
who wore bumper stickers on their gear —
love it or leave it —
that I would recall his image
while reading in The Daily News
about Moira Smith, wife, mother, officer
and dead at age thirty-nine on September 11, 2001
at ground zero — who, it turns out,
was no aspiring ingenue
but in her Our Lady of Angels uniform
appears for a few seconds playing handball
behind Travolta borrowing his friend's car.
There is no connection otherwise
between that Tuesday and Saturday Night Fever.
And my sorrow for her is incongruous
with grieving for that galaxy called youth.
(Were any of us once so hard and thin?) I am sorry
to even make this odd association. And the journalist
continued to state that her mortal remains
were conveyed from the WTC site

by fellow officers and that thirty police motorcycles
escorted her hearse to Our Lady of Lourdes Church
in Queens Village. I wish I could believe that
someone's remains might be mortal remains.
It sounds poetic and immortal.
More immortal than the movies.
She leaves behind a small daughter.

Kimiko Hahn

BOERUM HILL TANKA

24
Fathers and brothers still excavate and sift for the remains of the dead.
Hundreds. Across the water spring arrives: dutch elm, dogwood, cherry.
Immeasurably.

25
The beams of light memorializing the dead in this spring mist are not a
tourist attraction. Please. We see them every clear evening in Boerum Hill.

Patricia Spears Jones

ALL SAINTS DAY, 2001

The floating lights of the emergency vehicles circle wind.
We walk immune to Sirens shrieking.
What if the circling lights were pink or yellow, not blue and white?
Who is the Saint of fog?

                                    Who is the Saint of
our city decelerated in thick humidity, intemperate heat?

                                    Who is the Saint of
smiling eyed pretty girls wearing tiny heeled shoes and short skirts
prowling loud pubs on 2nd avenue or the gray hooded Black guys
smoking weed, talking trash in the shadows of Grand Central?

                                    Who is the Saint of
the Black woman in the pizza parlour who, after too many noise complaints
unheeded, declares "I own a 9 millimeter, legal,
if I shoot your dog what are you going to do about it?"

                                    Who is the Saint of
the boys in my "hood"
who call each other "son"
peer to peer father to father.

Where's daddy
where's mama
where's the good old days?

                        Is this the new catechism
and where is the handsome priest to answer?
By rote: do we sing a possible peace?

Shall we venture into this destroyed world thinking
charm, glee, proverbial opportunity

Shall we gather the names of the lost
then watch them float like feathers on the dirty wind

Shall we gather at the altars of old gods
and whine about our lives

                        Shall we watch the shadows watch us back

Now that clocks pulse instead of tick
are the streets safer for the wretched, the damned?

In what cinema are the dreams of mass destruction
so dear as ours?

Paul Violi

HOUSE OF XERXES

Here come those splendid Persians!
We were expecting fireworks
And here they are!
Short bows, long arrows,
Colorful long-sleeve shirts
Under iron breastplates —
Nice fish-scale pattern on those breastplates.
Just the right beach touch, very decky.
Quivers dangling under wicker-worky shields,
A casual touch, that.
And those floppy felt caps
Make it very wearable, very sporty.
Huge amounts of gold,
A killer-look feel
But it still says A Day at the Shore.

Now those bumping, thumping Assyrians.
A nice mix here: bronze helmets
Or plaited headgear.
Shields, spears, daggers,
The iron studs on those wooden clubs
A subtle retro bit.
And right on their heels the Bactrians!
A sort of butch-and-bitch combo,
Not tidy, not prim, almost
A dare-to-wear outfit.
And look at that headgear!

Whatever were they thinking?
And the bows, cane bows
Bringing back that beach scene scream.
Somebody's been smitten by cane.

Tromping right along: The Sacae!
Scythians with a scowl.
Plenty of flounce and pout but somehow
It all spells powerhouse.
Stiff, pointed helmets and loose trousers,
Bows, daggers, battleaxes:
Just look at these ratty party boys.
Itchy and raw, apocalyptic but functional.
Takes us away from the beach look
But how can you not love them?

Look at these Sarangae!
Are we ready for this?
Caspian jackets, cane bows,
This is the most colorful yet,
A lot of lavender, a lot of white and blue,
Colorama glamorama.
A little raggedy, a little trashy
Yet a narrow silhouette.
Narrow but masculine for sure.
Just what are these boys up to?

Oh, how can you not love
These madcap Ethiopians.
Leopard skins and lion pelts,
Long, long bows made of palm fronds.
Stone arrowheads, not iron, mind you.
And matching signet rings.
Details, details a must
If you want to gain that total look.
Spear heads made of gazelle horns.
Now that *is* a new twist.
And who thought of this — body paint!
Half white chalk, half ochre.
The all around mix and match
A big directional, indeed.

Check out the headgear!
A horse's scalp
Including ears and mane
For cryin' out loud.
The mane a crest, the ears stiff and upright
Very jaunty, very focused.
Somebody pinch me!

Now who's this?
Good grief, are we ready for the Libyans?
The brocade scaled back, thank god.
A big sulky leather look.

It's a bomber-jacket feeling.
I get a bomber-jacket feeling from this.
Javelins with burnt tips, daggers,
Minimal action gear but spiffy.

You don't want to miss this.
What a welcome
For the Paphlagonian cuties.
Marching, tromping right in.
Small shields, medium-length spears,
Javelins and daggers — overloaded
You might say, but
Why in heaven's name not?

Get a load of what's been done
With the traditional booties.
Half way up the shin.
A booty and greave combo.
Now how cute is that?
And everyone agrees
Under those plaited helmets
Those Paphlagonians
Have the curliest hair in the world.

Here come the Thracians.
Javelins, bucklets, small daggers.
Fox-skin caps, colorful tunics,

Fawn-skin boots, wooden helmets,
You just know how great
Their gorgeous garb makes them feel.

And right on their heels — the Pisidae.
Another wardrobe pick-me-up
With their small shields, two spears each,
And bronze helmets shaped
Into the ears and horns of an ox.
What a way to say: Surprise!

A very jaunty crest,
Red cloth wrapped around their legs,
Fashionable yet functional,
Smart but approachable,
Sporty in a tongue-in-chic sort of way.

You don't want to miss this!
Barefoot Sagartians, with lariats!
No optionals, nothing but lariats.
Now that is a new twist.
No fashion fears here.
The total look flouncy, loose and extra large.

Turbaned Cyprians
With high high high high greaves!
Wood bows, cane arrows

And goatskin capes — a cape
You could wear with anything.
Felt caps trimmed with feathers.
Dangling daggers, billhooks!
Untreated ox-hide vests.
Something we'd want in our closet.
Lion, tiger, fox and ox: the full idiom.
Upbeat and very wearable,
A dose of novelty, a dose
Of frivolity — a definite smash.

They are having a good time up there.
Rough and raw yet a lot of flash.
Lavish, zippy, sleek.
How can we take all this in?
Where is it all going?
An Etude for today's world.
A dressy apocalyptic beach look.
A high-octane action look.
A premium blend of guts
And sass and imagination.
Feel the frenzy.
A big round of applause for the whole spectrum,
For the very big directional
That can't help but whip it up.
Today we're making history.
We're raising cane.

Harvey Shapiro

BAD DAYS

If you can't say what you mean
then you might as well jump ship.
Like yesterday, even after
I had climbed the mountain,
I could not put Vermont together.
Spiritual heights are a downer
these days when what I need
is a jolt of real blue, and what I get
are piles of brown leaves
sliding by at a walker's pace.
Incremental evidence that something
is changing or is spooked and fleeing.

Harvey Shapiro

NIGHTS

Drunk and weeping. It's another
night at the live-in opera, and I figure
it's going to turn out badly for me.
The dead next door accept their salutations,
their salted notes, the drawn-out wailing.
It's we the living who must run for cover,
meaning me. Mortality's the ABC of it,
and after that comes lechery and lying.
And, oh, how to piece together a life
from this scandal and confusion, as if
the gods were inhabiting us or cohabiting
with us, just for the music's sake.

Anna Rabinowitz

BRICOLAGE: VERSICOLOR

All afternoon alterities advanced —
    afars abdicated —
        and azure anons abandoned the air —

        and

Beyond blue — betrayal, blasphemy, brimstone, and bray —

       blind bards' bereaved ballads beached
            on bygones of bearded beliefs —

COULD WE HAVE CALLED FOR A CESSATION OF CLAMORS —

    COULD WE HAVE CAUTIONED
        CRIMSON NOT TO COLONIZE ITS CAKES
        ON CATAFALQUES OF

DUN — to defy the doomsayers — those

    deathdealing   dreaddroning   dreardoting

       drillmerchants of dark —

Entropy and elans of eclipse —
        emerald and the envy of ecru —

Fractured fuschias fueled
    by frontmen flexed for the fray —

       flash-frozen futures

Gone glottal   gone global

      O grizzly graffiti
          grassed in gray grammar —

      O grim geography

Hounding the heliotrope horoscope —
        hardworking harbinger —
           our hyacinth of hope —

Inland ideologies infected incunabula
        infernos ignited innuendo
     and ironies injected ivory in inks —

January Juned —
    jardins jammed —
      jonquils jealous for

Knowledge of khaki and kohl knotted in kow-tows
           to karma and ken —

Lavender let legions —
        lavender leered —
               lavender lured leitmotifs landward to

Mollify maverick mauves —
        the marl and the maelstrom —

      masked mayhem of markets
           mazed and marooned

Now noted for necromancing the navy nostalgias of the
        numberless numerous
           numbed by the nonce of night's noon —

ONSLAUGHT OF OCHRE, ONTOGENY OF OBLIVION —

        oracular omens

Polluted by postscripts of paid product placement
        and puce pandemonium plundered the port —

Quotidians quaquaed quite quixotically —
        quests quaked and

quinced the quays —

Ruby rode rain—

READER   IS THIS RHETORIC OR REALISM

REDDENED AND ROUGED —

STRAPHANGERS

ARE WE SCARLET OR SEPIA
SURFSURGE OR SLAM —

ARE WE SELLER OR SOLD —

Trophy the true —
          tango the traipse —
                    tidy the taupe —
                                        O terrestrial tourists

Unumber ulterior's unanimous urge —

Very vermilion the virtual void —
                    valiant the verge —

Weltschmerz of weathers —

woundweary whites —

whither our windows
our wardrobes   our warbles   our woos

whilst

Xanadu xanthenes and X xes X —

Yammer yes yammer yes yowlyelp
           you yellowedyearyesteryore yields

yonder yearn yarrow
           and yodeling yews
       yonder young
Zinnias zaffer the zeds —

ZEITGEIST   MY ZEITGEIST   ZUPPA DI ZOOS (ZEUS)

ZERO, O ZERO, OUR ZEALOTSTREWN ZONES —

George Murray

THE STATUE

Suddenly the statuary is upon us,
hovering with panicked airs —
why didn't we notice it sneaking up?

Guilt has unexpectedly become tangible,
is falling from its bearers
in tears of marble and limestone —

shall we rebuild the cracked white pillars,
the chipped plinths?
Shall we quarry here in the light

and air above ground? Free
of the weight of fault
might we finally shoot into the sky

as we were obviously destined to?
Or, without ballast,
will we tip at the crest of the next wave?

What is the danger of speaking
against this in one's head?
That someone might be listening?

It was a good but rocky world
as recently as yesterday —
it is there to see in all the papers of record,

in all the shadows painted on the walls
of our caves. What was bound
to happen? This. Despite how unlikely

the events of our Fall may have seemed,
there was always
a hundred percent chance

things would turn out this way. Prophecy,
it seems, is almost always just
an unrestrained case of History envy.

Alicia Ostriker

THE WINDOW, AT THE MOMENT OF FLAME

and all this while I have been playing with toys
a toy superhighway a toy automobile a house of blocks

and all this while far off in other lands
thousands and thousands, millions and millions

you know — you see the pictures
women carrying bony infants

men sobbing over graves
buildings sculpted by explosion —

earth wasted bare and rotten
and all this while I have been shopping, I have

been let us say free
and do they hate me for it

do they hate *me*

D. Nurkse

OCTOBER MARRIAGE

I

We dial a recording
and order Vitamin K,
Cipro, twin masks.

Shunted between prompts,
we stare at each other
with deep longing,
drumming our fingers
while the line grows faint.

We borrow a Glock and wrap it
in a Chamois cloth and lock
the bullets in a separate drawer —
where to hang the key?

We stockpile Poland Spring
under our bed
and feel that bulk
nullify the give
when we make love.

2

Huddled before the news,
we touch the screen —
our bombs rain on Kandahar —
we can't feel them:
just a thrum, the pulse,

a film of dust, a red glow
shining through our nails.

3
We saw it
and can't stop watching:
as if the plane entered the eye
and it was the mind
that began burning
with such a stubborn flame.

We saw the bodies jump
and couldn't break their fall —
now they wait so gracefully
in midair, holding hands.

David Lehman

9/14/01

Before September 11
I would have written it
one way. I would have
interviewed the soldier
who volunteers to die
as penance for his part
in the erotic shipwreck.
He had understood her
as little as she had
understood him though
there were children
to consider and now
they were orphans.
I would have depicted
the plane crash as an
accident in a world of
disorder not a careful
calculation. But now
they love us, because
we've taken this hit,
and in case you forget
all you have to do is
look up and it's not there.

David Lehman

9/15/01

I shall draw a broken tower
as once I drew the Tower
in a Tarot reading. A man
shaving sees in the mirror
a dog howling in a storm
and we climb the tower
and get dizzy as we near
the top where nuns appear
and a woman jumps to her
death then does it again
and the lightning meant
the crisis was here and
here is where I wanted
no place I'd sooner be.

Rachel Hadas

TANGERINE ORCHIDS

These flowers unlock a heart I hadn't known
was locked; mend what I didn't know was broken.
That much was broken I did know. But me?
I hadn't dreamed, as some of my friends had,
of bombs and masked intruders,
doomed flailings at escape. I had not seen
the double horror happen over and over.
I'd simply tried to live a little. Not
"closure," not "moving on."
Where was there to move to?
October light, the river, and my city:
staying, not moving, seemed to be the theme.
But then if staying means a holding on
to what is gone, there is no staying either.
Each time I pass them, faces pull at me
and I am no exception. Multiply
my little pain by millions — there it is,
the wound, mine too, but wound I had ignored
until these foxy flowers opened it.
Brought into view, the wound began to bleed.
What we can see, we mourn for, and rejoice
that we can mourn. Not mourn and then rejoice;
mourn and rejoice at once.

Care Tips, the glossy sheet accompanying these orchids,
advises: "Trim 1/2 an inch or more
from each spray and submerge entire stem,

blossoms and all, in fresh room temperature water."
Have I been cut? These flowers are bathing me
in water not much warmer than room temperature
and salt, not fresh. But tears, however salt,
are sweet. In Homer they all know that. Dickens
in a newly published letter writes:
The cultivation of little gardens,
if they be no bigger than graves,
is a great resource and a great reward.
These tangerine orchids are a resource.
The city is a garden and a grave.

Rachel Hadas

SUNDAY AFTERNOON

Recollection of what's been lost;
gradual sifting away
of what had hung around
accumulating, ripening for years
until the time arrived for it to go:
pumice stones from France, Greek worry beads
coming unstrung, ceramic fish whose tail
long ago broke off, dead tennis balls —
each item from a different layer of past
life stratifying into history
whose catalog, like any
list, is open ended.

Surely human lives,
the lives of those we love
or even those we don't
outweigh the value of
a mildewed quilt, a tattered T-shirt
with a familiar smell.
But do they? When ourselves will turn to ash,
scattered, if we are lucky,
above the gardens we ourselves have planted,
sprinkled on the waters we have sailed,
will we be more than broken knickknacks then,
dispensable as everything becomes
with time, but also stowed away as safely
as anything can be
that is locked up in memory?

These thoughts,
soft and porous as the puffy clouds
sailing across a stippled sky, subside
into default mode, our native state —
uncertainty. Some answer may be floating
past; I am abstracted,
sitting on a boulder by the river,
Sunday afternoon, September ninth.

Knowledge can only look
back over her shoulder.
The grey-green Hudson with its faint salt smell
laps at the stones. Look up: a fat red blimp
sails slowly south. Behind me,
felled by sleepiness,
picnickers on the grass
sprawl like courtiers in The Sleeping Beauty
among half-finished crossword
puzzles. Babies in their strollers look
more alert than their elders.
And here's the blimp again — so soon! Can it
have sailed clear down to the Battery already
and seeing that all was well
this drowsy afternoon
come nosing mildly as a manatee
northward again?

Nikki Moustaki

HOW TO WRITE A POEM AFTER
SEPTEMBER 11TH

First: Don't use the word *souls*. Don't use the word *fire*.
You can use the word *tragic* if you end it with a k.
The rules have changed. The word *building* may precede
The word *fall*, but only in the context of the buildings falling
Before the fall, the season we didn't have in Manhattan
Because the weather refused, the air refused...
Don't say the air smelled like smoldering desks and drywall,
Ground gypsum, and something terribly organic,
Don't make a metaphor about the smell, because it wasn't
A smell at all, but the air washed with working souls,
Piling bricks, one by one, spreading mortar.
Don't compare the planes to birds. Please.
Don't call the windows eyes. We know they saw it coming.
We know they didn't blink. Don't say they were sentinels.
Say: we hated them then we loved them then they were gone.
Say: we miss them. Say: there's a gape. Then, say something
About love. It's always good in a poem to mention love.
Say: If a man walks down stairs, somewhere
Another man is walking up. Say: He sits at his desk
And the other stands. He answers the phone and the other
Ends a call with a kiss. So, on a rainy dusk in some other
City of Commerce and Art, a mayor cuts a ribbon
With giant silver scissors. Are you writing this down?
Make the executives parade through the concourse,
Up the elevators, to the top, where the restaurant,
Open now for the first time, sets out a dinner buffet.
Press hard. Remember, you're writing with ashes.

Say: the phone didn't work. Say: the bakery was out of cake,
The dogs in the pound howled. Say: the world hadn't
Asked your permission to change. But you were asleep.
If you had only written more poems. If only you had written
More poems about love, about peace, about how abstractions
Become important outside the poem, outside. Then, then,
You could have squinted into the sky on September 11th
And said: thank you, thank you, nothing was broken today.

Ron Drummond

AS ZEUS

I would've intervened
to shield you from those sights,
those screams, that horrific dust.
A dazzling mist, I'd have swept you

up the Hudson, north to the river's
narrower reaches, then safely down
to a mountain lake, to a vacant canoe.
I'd have been that vessel's able oars.

I'd have been the fir trees bent
in greeting. I'd have been
a train of nine or ten mergansers,
each puckish diver more showy

than the other, our red pompadours
slick as we'd come up for air.
You'd have leapt into my
almost-autumn water, and I'd

have been the towel that teased
a smile above your dimpled chin.
And maybe I would've turned
into a flock of wild geese out

for an evening saunter.
But after a concert in coyote
and loon-song, I'd have winged you
home, become a shower;

soaped you, rinsed you, prepared
you for bed, where I'd have gladly
given up my godhood.
Our mortal arms would have

held each other's mortal flesh,
would've braced our fall for change.

Geoffrey O'Brien

AUBADE 2

Hysteria of morning. A clearing, the half-gnawed
bones of last night's feast, a cry in the ravine.
There is too much smoke in the jungle, or not enough.
Nothing fits, nothing is quite right. Pieces of cloud-cover
litter the overgrown path. It's as if no one
had ever lived here, yet we still have to get up
to find wood. Neurasthenia of morning. The clearing
breaks down into bands of colors, the violent greens
soothed by outbursts of red. It's patched itself
together once again, even if the sky
is still partly ripped. The cracks in the burnt bones
seem almost pictures of roads. The roads
are so much like burnt bones I regret that the day
even at this early hour is no longer black.

Geoffrey O'Brien

THE BED IN THE WILDERNESS

The magic bed
is found in a cave

or falls like a hammock
from the sky.

Its fringes glisten.
It invites the lost traveler.

To sleep in it is to roll
in a dream of treasure,

to wake in it to lose
all taste for treasure.

Geoffrey O'Brien

TECHNIQUES OF MASS PERSUASION

Freedom is the ability to admit you were wrong.
Sorry, kids, I sold the farm so we can move to a suburb
of Antioch. I'm so glad I didn't. There are second acts
in American lives, and third and fourth ones.
After his release from prison he became a food taster
for a large department store. He had already written
the book on which his own letters home were based.
Freedom is the capacity to remember that it's a movie
even when the mansion starts burning in the last reel.
To unsettle without disturbing, to shift the candle
in the window to produce a will-o'-the-wisp effect
even from a great distance, these are techniques
calculated to persuade no one of anything.
As they leave the theater they savor their freedom.

Tim Suermondt

SQUAD I

The boy parks his red fire engine,
removes his red fireman's hat
and rests against the bedpost —
it was a rough, dangerous day
on the job
but everyone was saved
from the inferno
no one died
and all the firemen came out,
small birds on each
of their massive shoulders.

Tim Suermondt

MISSING SUPPER

Don't grieve too long
over the ones who will never
be with us for another meal.
Rest assured that wherever they are

they are cooking a simple
and nourishing meal and parading
now and then in wide aprons
embossed with the words

IF THE POT BOILS, FRIENDSHIP LIVES.
They've saved us a place at their table
and are relishing the chance
when they can escort us into the kitchen

and fill us in on all the mysteries, answers
flowing from their lips sweetly as fine wine.
Blow out the candles and turn on the stove —
how beautiful we were, how beautiful we are.

MIRANDA BEESON'S poems have appeared in literary journals such as *Barrow Street* and *The Malahat Review*. She is a long-time resident of New York's Chelsea neighborhood.

STAR BLACK is the author of four books of poems: *Double Time* (Ground Water), *Waterworn* (Fly By Night), *October for Idas* and *Balefire* (both from Painted Leaf). She is also co-director of the popular poetry reading series at the KGB Bar in Manhattan's East Village. Born in Coronado, California and raised in Washington D.C. and Hawaii, she now lives in Midtown Manhattan.

ANDREA CARTER BROWN'S *Brooke & Rainbow* won the 2000 Sow's Ear Press Chapbook Competition. Her poems have appeared in *Ploughshares, The Mississippi Review, The Gettysburg Review* and elsewhere. A founding editor of *Barrow Street*, she was displaced from her home in Battery Park City by the events of September 11 but has since moved back.

RON DRUMMOND'S poetry has appeared in such literary publications as the *Northwest Review, Borderlands, Global City Review, Columbia Review, The Journal, Phoebe, Poetry New York,* and *Poetry Nation*. A founding editor of the poetry journal *Barrow Street*, he lives in Chelsea.

STEPHEN DUNN is the author of twelve collections of poetry, including *Different Hours* (winner of the 2001 Pulitzer Prize), and the forthcoming *Local Visitations*, both from W.W. Norton. He grew up in Queens, lived in Greenwich Village, and now makes his home in New Jersey.

PHILIP FRIED has published two books of poetry, *Mutual Trespasses* (Ion Books) and *Quantum Genesis* (Koen). His latest manuscript is *Big Men Speaking to Little Men*. He lives on Manhattan's Upper West Side.

DOUGLAS GOETSCH'S latest collection of poems, *What's Worse*, won the 2001 Aldrich Chapbook Prize. He is also the author of *Nobody's Hell* (Hanging Loose) and *Wherever You Want* (Pavement). He teaches creative writing to incarcerated teens in the South Bronx, and lives in Greenwich Village.

RACHEL HADAS is the author of 12 books of poetry, essays and translations, including *Halfway Down the Hall: New and Selected Poems*, and her most recent collection, *Indelible*, both from Wesleyan. The recipient of a Guggenheim Fellowship, she is also a member of the American Academy of Arts and Sciences. She teaches at Rutgers University (Newark) and lives on the Upper West Side.

KIMIKO HAHN's seven collections include *The Artist's Daughter,* and *Mosquito and Ant* (both W.W. Norton), *Volatile* (Hanging Loose) and *The Unbearable Heart* (Kaya), which was awarded an American Book Award. She has received fellowships from the National Endowment for the Arts and the Lila Wallace-Reader's Digest Fund and is a professor at Queens College/CUNY. She lives in Brooklyn.

SCOTT HIGHTOWER is the author of *Tin Can Tourist* (Fordham University Press). His work has also appeared in *Ploughshares, Salmagundi, The Yale Review* and *AGNI.* He is a contributing editor of *The Journal,* and teaches at New York University/Gallatin. He lives in Chelsea.

VICKI HUDSPITH is the author of *White and Nervous* (Bench Press) and *Limousine Dreams,* published with drawings by James DeWoody. She is President of the Board of Directors of The Poetry Project in New York City. Her poetry has appeared in numerous small press magazines. She lives in Manhattan's Tribeca neighborhood.

COLETTE INEZ is the author of eight books of poetry, including most recently *Clemency* (Carnegie Mellon, 1998). She is a two-time Pushcart Prize winner, and has received fellowships from the New York State Foundation for the Arts, the Guggenheim and Rockefeller Foundations, and twice from the National Endowment for the Arts. She is on the faculty of Columbia University's Writing Program and lives on the Upper West Side.

PATRICIA SPEARS JONES is the author of *The Weather That Kills* (Coffee House Press) and co-editor of the anthology *Ordinary Women* (Ordinary Women Books). Her poems have appeared in *Best American Poetry 2000, Blood and Tears: Poems for Matthew Shepard,* and *Sisterfire: An Anthology of Black Women's Writing.* She teaches at Parson's School of Design, and lives in Brooklyn.

ELIOT KATZ is the author of *Unlocking the Exits* (Coffee House Press) and *Space and Other Poems* (Northern Lights), and a co-editor of *Poems for the Nation* (Seven Stories Press), a collection of contemporary political poems compiled by the late poet Allen Ginsberg. Katz is also a cofounder and former coeditor of the literary magazine *Long Shot.* He lives in Astoria, Queens.

KARL KIRCHWEY was Director of the 92nd Street Y Unterberg Poetry Center in New York City from 1987-2000. He has received the Ingram Merrill Award, National Endowment for the Arts and Guggenheim fellowships, and the Rome Prize in Literature. His fourth books of poems, *At the Palace of Jove* (Putnam) will be published in October 2002. He lives on the Upper West Side.

SHARON KRAUS is the author of *Generation* (Wesleyan) and *Strange Land* (University Press of Florida), a finalist for the 2000 National Poetry Series. Her work has appeared in *Puerto del Sol, Quarterly West, Agni, The Mississippi Review* and elsewhere. Her awards include the Editors' Choice award from Columbia and fellowships from the MacDowell Colony. She lives in Montclair, New Jersey.

BILL KUSHNER is the author of *Love Uncut* and *Head* (both from United Artists) and *Night Fishing* (Midnight Sun Press). He is a 1999 winner of a New York Foundation of the Arts Award, and his work will appear in *Best American Poetry 2002*, guest-edited by Robert Creeley. He lives in Chelsea.

ANNE-MARIE LEVINE is the author of *Euphorbia* (Provincetown Arts Press), a finalist for the Paterson Poetry Prize. Her poems have appeared in *Parnassus, Tin House, Crossconnect,* and elsewhere. A member of the Board of Directors of Poets House and a founder of the Poets & Performers reading series, she lives on the Upper East Side.

DAVID LEHMAN is the author of five books of poetry, including *The Evening Sun* and *The Daily Mirror* (both from Scribner). His most recent nonfiction books are *The Last Avant-Garde: The Making of the New York School of Poets* (Doubleday) and the revised edition of *The Perfect Murder: A Study in Detection* (University of Michigan). He lives within walking distance of Washington Square Park.

FRANK LIMA is the author of five books of poetry, the most recent of which are *Inventory: New and Selected Poems* and *The Beatitudes* (both from Hard Press), and his poetry has been widely anthologized. Born in Spanish Harlem and trained in classical French cooking, he is currently a Chef Instructor at The Art Institute of New York. He lives in Flushing, Queens.

ROSS MARTIN is poetry editor for Nerve.com, and recently published his first book, *The Cop Who Rides Alone* (Zoo Press). His work has appeared in *Boulevard,* the *Kenyon Review, Prairie Schooner* and elsewhere. A former development executive for Spike Lee's 40 Acres & A Mule Filmworks, he teaches poetry at The New School. He lives in Murray Hill.

NANCY MERCADO is the author of the collection *It Concerns The Madness* (Long Shot Productions, 2000). Her work has also been anthologized in *Role Call* (Third World Press), *ALOUD: Voices from the Nuyorican Poets Café* (Henry Holt) and *Bum Rush the Page* (Random House). An editor of the literary journal *Long Shot*, she resides on the Upper West Side.

NIKKI MOUSTAKI is the recipient of a National Endowment for the Arts fellowship in poetry for 2001, and is the author of *The Complete Idiot's Guide to Writing Poetry*. She lives in the Hell's Kitchen neighborhood in Manhattan.

GEORGE MURRAY's most recent book is *The Cottage Builder's Letter* (McClelland and Stewart). His poems have also appeared in *The Iowa Review, The Mid-American Review, Pequod,* and others journals. He works just south of the World Trade Center, at the corner of Washington and Rector Streets, and was at the scene on September 11th. He escaped the rain of debris with minor injuries. He lives in Washington Heights.

EILEEN MYLES is a poet who lives in NY and a novelist who teaches at University of California, San Diego. She is the author of several books of fiction, non-fiction and poetry. Her most recent poetry books are *Skies* (Black Sparrow, 2001) and *on my way* (Faux Press, 2001). She lives on the Lower East Side.

D. NURKSE is the Poet Laureate of Brooklyn, and author of seven books of poetry, including most recently *The Fall* (Knopf) as well as *Leaving Xaia, The Rules of Paradise,* and *Voices Over Water* (all from Four Way Books). His poems have recently been featured in *The New Yorker* and in *Best American Poetry 2002*. He lives in Brooklyn.

GEOFFREY O'BRIEN's books include the collections *A Book of Maps, The Hudson Mystery* (both from Red Dust*)*, and *Floating City: Selected Poems 1978-1995* (Talisman House). He is editor-in-chief of The Library of America and contributes frequently to *The New York Review of Books, Artforum,* and other publications. Born in New York City, he was displaced from his home in Battery Park City for four months by the events of September 11.

ALICIA OSTRIKER is the author of ten volumes of poetry, including *The Crack in Everything* (1996) and *The Little Space: Poems Selected and New, 1968-1998,* both finalists for the National Book Award, and *The Imaginary Lover* (1986), winner of the William Carlos Williams Award (all from University of Pittsburgh). Her most recent book is *The Volcano Sequence* (University of Pittsburgh 2002). She lives in New Jersey.

MOLLY PEACOCK is Poet-in-Residence at Manhattan's Cathedral of St. John the Divine. She is the author of *Cornucopia: New & Selected Poems* (Norton), *How To Read A Poem & Start A Poetry Circle* (Putnam), and a memoir, *Paradise Piece By Piece* (Putnam). She is one of the creators of Poetry in Motion, a program to place poetry on New York City's subways and buses. She lives in the East Village.

ANNA RABINOWITZ is the publisher and editor of *American Letters & Commentary*. Her books include *Darkling: A Poem* (Tupelo Press, 2001) and *At the Site of Inside Out*, (University of Massachusetts, 1997). Her awards include an National Endowment for the Arts grant and the Juniper Prize. She is a life-long New Yorker, born in Brooklyn and now residing on the Upper East Side.

CARTER RATCLIFF, a contributing editor of *Art in America*, is the author of two books of poetry, *Fever Coast* (Kulchur Press) and *Give Me Tomorrow* (Vehicle Press), and numerous books on art, including, most recently, *Out of the Box: The Reinvention of Art, 1965-1975* (Allworth Press). His essay collection, *The Figure of the Artist,* is forthcoming from Cambridge University Press. He lives six blocks from the site of the World Trade Center.

PHILIP SCHULTZ is the author of *The Holy Worm of Praise* (Harcourt) and *Deep Within the Ravine* and *Like Wings* (both Viking). He has received an American Academy of Art and Letters Award, a Lamont Prize and *Poetry*'s Levinson Prize. He founded and directs The Writers Studio in New York City and lives in East Hampton.

HUGH SEIDMAN's first book *Collecting Evidence* won the Yale Series of Younger Poets Prize, and his newest, *Selected Poems: 1965-1995* (Miami University) was named among the best books of 1995 by the *Village Voice* and by *The Critics Choice*. He has taught at the University of Wisconsin, Yale University, Columbia University, and the New School University. Born in Brooklyn, he now lives in the West Village.

HARVEY SHAPIRO's most recent book is *How Charlie Shavers Died and Others Poems*, published by Wesleyan in 2001. He is also the author of *The Light Holds* and *New and Selected Poems,* also from Wesleyan, and *A Day's Portion* (Hanging Loose). He is a senior editor of *The New York Times Magazine*, and has lived in Brooklyn Heights for over forty years.

HAL SIROWITZ is the Poet Laureate of Queens and Slam Champ of the Nuyorican Café's 1st Poetry Festival. He is the author of the collections *Mother Said* and *My Therapist Said* (both from Crown). He teaches elementary special education in the New York City Public School system, and lives in Flushing.

AARON SMITH's poems have appeared in *5 AM, Kestrel, Pearl* and elsewhere. He has been awarded an Academy of American Poets Prize from the University of Pittsburgh, and is the recipient of the 1998 Kestrel Poetry Prize. He moved to New York City on August 6, 2001 and lives in the East Village.

CHARLIE SMITH is the author of five books of poetry, including, *Before and After, The Palms*, and most recently, *Heroin: And Other Poems* (all from Norton), as well as six novels, including *Shine Hawk* (Paris Review Editions). He is the recipient of grants from the National Endowment for the Arts and the Guggenhiem Foundation. He lives in Greenwich Village.

SHELLEY STENHOUSE's collection *Pants* won the 1999 Pavement Saw Press Chapbook Award. She also won the 2000 Allen Ginsberg award and a 2001 New York Foundation for the Arts fellowship. Her poems have appeared in *The Antioch Review, Prairie Schooner, Quarterly West, Paterson Review*, and *Mudfish*. She has lived in Greenwich Village for 22 years.

NORMAN STOCK's collection *Buying Breakfast for MY Kamikaze Pilot* was published by Gibbs Smith in 1994 as winner of the Peregrine Smith Poetry Contest. His work has also appeared in numerous literary publications, including *The New Republic, College English, The New York Quarterly*, and *Verse*. He lives in Jackson Heights, Queens.

TIM SUERMONDT's work has appeared in journals such as *Poetry Northwest, Barrow Street*, and the *Cortland Review*, among others, and he is the author of two books: *The Dangerous Women With Their Cellos* (Manny Trio Press) and *Greatest Hits 1988-2001* (Pudding House Press). He lives in Jamaica, Queens.

TONY TOWLE is the author of 10 books of poetry, most recently *The History of the Invitation: New and Selected Poems 1963-2000* (Hanging Loose Press). His book *Memoir 1960-63* (Faux Press), published in 2001, was fortuitously completed and sent to the publisher on September 10, 2001. A Manhattan resident for 41 years, he lives in Tribeca, eleven blocks north of the World Trade Center site.

DAVID TRINIDAD's newest collection, *Plasticville* (Turtle Point Press), was a finalist for the Lenore Marshall Poetry Prize. His other books include *Answer Song* (High Risk/Serpent's Tail) and *Pavane* (Sherwood). His work has also appeared in *American Poetry Review, Harper's, The Paris Review* and *Postmodern American Poetry: A Norton Anthology*. He teaches in the MFA Writing Program at the New School, and lives in Soho.

JEAN VALENTINE is the author of eight books of poetry, including her first book, *Dream Barker,* which won the Yale Series of Younger Poets Prize, as well as *The Messenger* (Farrar, Straus & Giroux) and, most recently, *The Cradle of the Real Life* (Wesleyan, 2000). She lives and works in Manhattan.

PAUL VIOLI is a recipient of the 2001 Morton Dauwen Zabel Poetry Award from the American Academy of Arts and Letters. His books include *Fracas* and *Likewise* (both Hanging Loose) and *Breakers* (Coffee House).He teaches at Columbia and New York University. He has worked in Manhattan since he was a teenager, and lives just north of the city in Putnam Valley.

LEWIS WARSH is the author of over twenty-five books of poetry, fiction and autobiography, including the recent collections *Ted's Favorite Skirt* (Spuyten Duyvil), and *The Origin of the World* (Creative Arts). He is on the faculty of Long Island University and lives in Greenpoint, Brooklyn.

ABOUT THE EDITORS:

DENNIS LOY JOHNSON has been the recipient of a Pushcart Prize and a National Endowment for the Arts fellowship for his short fiction. His work has appeared in *Ploughshares*, *The Georgia Review*, *The New England Review* and elsewhere, and in anthologies such as *The New Generation* (Doubleday / Anchor), and *New Stories from the South* (Algonquin). He lives in Hoboken, New Jersey.

VALERIE MERIANS is a visual artist whose work is shown in New York City. She studied poetry at the Iowa Writer's Workshop at The University of Iowa, where she co-founded and co-edited the literary magazine, *Luna Tack*. She has reviewed fiction and poetry for newspapers including *The Milwaukee Journal-Sentinel* and *The Pittsburgh Tribune-Review*. She lives in Hoboken, New Jersey.

ACKNOWLEDGEMENTS

The editors wish to thank Alicia Ostriker for her help and inspiration on this project. We are also indebted to Heléne Aylon, Star Black, Denise Duhamel, David Lehman and Hal Sirowitz for their advice and assistance in contacting poets. And to all the many poets who sent us work we were unable to include, we send heartfelt thanks. It was nonetheless inspiring. This book represents just the tip of the iceberg.